THIS BOOK BELONGS TO:

_____

DEAR PARENTS AND TEACHERS,

We have been conditioned to reassure children that their fears are not real, that monsters do not hide in closets, that it's easy to speak in front of a group or to make new friends. But those fears are very real to children.

Yes, children need to be reassured when anxious, but what is equally, if not more important, is that they internalize reassurance and feel a sense of power over their fears. Teaching children to develop a healthy internal strength will boost confidence and will reassure them that they can handle each new, anxious situation they encounter.

This book demonstrates a simple and effective technique called the *Magic Finger Countdown* which is rooted in Cognitive Behavioral Therapy and Acceptance and Commitment Therapy. The technique is used for conquering fear in almost any situation—from staying in a big kid bed at night, to imaginary monsters in the closet, to talking in front of a group.

Children do not have to live with debilitating fear and anxiety. Behavior can be changed, and anxiety can be transformed into a sense of personal power.

Read this book with your children or students, explore the Afterword for tips on implementing the technique, and encourage children to try the *Magic Finger Countdown* in any situation where they feel afraid.

Stacy Fiorile and
Barry McDonagh

Summary: Teaches school age children how to overcome
the debilitating anxiety and panic worry-cycle.

For more information on Barry's work visit www.panicaway.com
For more information on Stacy's work visit www.panicaway.com/kids

Disclaimer: This book is provided for informational purposes only. This book is not intended as
a substitute for the medical advice of physicians or intended as a substitute for professional help
or therapy. The reader should regularly consult a physician in matters relating to his/her health,
particularly with respect to any symptoms that may require diagnosis or medical attention.
Licensed health care professionals must assess the diagnosis and treatment of any symptoms
or related health conditions. Be sure to have your child evaluated by a physician to rule-out
any underlying medical conditions.

Publisher's Cataloging-In-Publication Data
(Prepared by The Donohue Group, Inc.)

Fiorile, Stacy L.
   Scaredies away! : a kid's guide to overcoming worry and anxiety (made simple) /
Stacy L. Fiorile, MA, CAGS, NJCSP, NCSP (Nationally Certified School Psychologist) and Barry
McDonagh, BA, Dip Psych., best selling author of Panic Away ; edited by Angelle Pilkington ;
illustrations and cover design by Denis Alonso ; interior book design by Solari Creative.
-- First edition.

      pages : colored illustrations ; cm

   Summary: Eight-year-old Jack is scared of the dark, of swimming in the ocean, and of
riding the biggest roller coaster on the boardwalk. Jack usually runs away from what scares
him. But now that his cousin Clay has taught him how to overcome his fears all on his own,
Jack is ready to take on the world! Includes basics of the Magic Finger Countdown
technique and tips for success.
   Interest age level: 006-012.
   ISBN: 978-0-9565962-4-6
   ISBN: 978-0-615-98914-3
   ISBN: 978-1-4960-2040-6

1. Fear in children--Juvenile fiction. 2. Anxiety in children--Juvenile fiction. 3. Roller coasters--
Juvenile fiction. 4. Fear--Fiction. 5. Anxiety--Fiction. 6. Roller coasters--Fiction. I. McDonagh,
Barry. II. Pilkington, Angelle. III. Alonso, Denis, 1986- IV. Solari Creative (Firm) V. Title.

PZ7.F49871 Sc 2014
[Fic]   2014905141

FOR MY TWO BEAUTIFUL CHILDREN

Thank you to my two little inspirations and to
my most amazing and supportive husband, Rob.
And of course, thank you, Barry. ~SF

FOR SOPHIA AND REJANE

Thanks to Regan, Brenda, Lilly, Sive, Angelina, Patrick,
Rejane and Sophia for their invaluable feedback. ~BMD

Scaredies Away!

A Kid's Guide to
Overcoming Worry and
Anxiety (made simple)

by Stacy L. Fiorile, MA, CAGS, NJCSP, NCSP (Nationally Certified School Psychologist) and Barry McDonagh, BA, Dip Psych., best selling author of *Panic Away*.

BMD Publishing LTD

Edited by Angelle Pilkington

Illustrations and cover design by Denis Alonso

Interior book design by Solari Creative

CRASH!

A huge wave rolled
and tumbled ashore.

"Aak!" Jack dodged toward drier
sand while his cousin, Clay, surfed
the wave all the way in.

8

"Awesome," Jack whispered. It was the first day at the shore with his parents, sister, aunts, uncles, and cousins. Jack had spent the morning watching Clay surf. Jack really wished he were brave enough to surf like his big cousin.

Clay speared his surfboard into the sand. "Perfect waves today, but I'm beat. Hey, how about we go to the boardwalk and ride Big Red? It'll be wild!" Jack gulped. The only thing scarier than the ocean was

BIG RED!

9

Jack and Clay filed into the long line for Big Red. Jack stared up at the humongous, old, wooden roller coaster. He couldn't believe his parents were letting him ride it. Jack wondered if Clay could tell he was scared?

"It'll be just like riding a wave," Clay said.

OU MUST BE THIS TALL

10

I guess he can tell I'm afraid, Jack thought. He was embarrassed. He could only nod. His legs suddenly felt like wobbly noodles, and his tummy felt tight.

"Hey, can you keep a secret?" Clay asked, and Jack nodded again. "I used to be afraid of surfing the big waves."

11

"No way!" Jack couldn't believe that Clay had ever been afraid of anything.

"Yep. I was scared of the waves—and Big Red!—until an old surf pro taught me the MFC. Magic Finger Countdown." Clay and Jack were both quiet for a minute as they shuffled forward in line.

12

"Want me to tell you how it works?" Clay finally asked.

"Will it make it easier for me to ride Big Red too?" Jack asked.

"Uh-huh. It works on killer waves, humongous roller coasters, monsters in closets, and anything else that's scary," replied Clay.

13

14

Clay passed through the ride's first turnstile, and Jack followed. "All right," Clay began. "The first thing to know is that *everyone*—even surf pros and cousins and your parents—get scared sometimes. And no one ever tells you that it's totally OK not to feel OK sometimes."

Jack tried to swallow, but his throat was dry, and he coughed.

Clay patted him on the back. "Dude, if you want to feel better, first thing to do is make fun of your scaredies."

"Wh-wh-what?" Jack stammered. How could he make fun of his own feelings?

"Scaredies can't hurt you; they're just feelings. Treat them like your goofiest friend—or cousin. Like right now my stomach feels funky with butterflies, but I know I'm safe, so I just say, 'Hell-ooooo butterflies. Come on in! The more the merrier! Have a party in there for me!" Clay explained.

Clay made a goofy face, and both boys burst out laughing.

"OK, I can do that." Jack replied.

16

"Next you go like this"—Clay closed one hand into a fist—"and you put all your scaredies right in there like they're all being laser-beamed from your body, into your arm, and then into your mighty fist of fury!"

Jack laughed again. Clay really was his goofiest cousin.

"You keep all that locked in your fist for as long as you want, bro." Clay squeezed his fist tight. "And you tell those scaredies that you are *not* scared of *them* anymore."

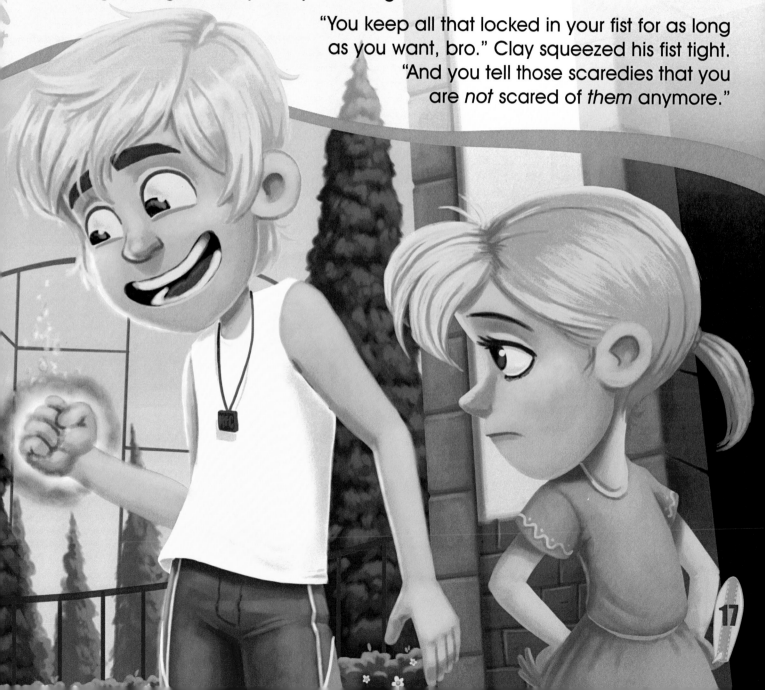

17

The boys were almost to the front of the line. Jack could even see the little red cars they would sit in.

"OK, Jack. When you're ready, you have to set those scaredies free. So you let go of one finger at a time"—Clay lifted his thumb—"and count each finger out nice and slow

five ... four ... three ... two ... one."

BIG

Jack nodded, listening.

Clay continued. "And then blow on it to make sure it's all outta there." Clay gave three quick puffs on his open hand and said, "See ya, scaredies. Get lost."

19

"**YOU'RE NEXT!**" a tall, grouchy-looking ride attendant shouted at the boys. Jack could feel his eyes go saucer-wide. "Dude, try the Magic Finger Countdown (MFC). It seriously works," Clay said.

"O-O-OK," Jack said. He looked around to see if anyone was watching them, then started with a whisper. "Hello, icky tummy." Then he tried as hard as he could to squeeze all those scared feelings into his fist. He counted down, releasing one finger at a time. "Five, four, three, two, one." He blew on his hand and said good-bye to his scaredies.

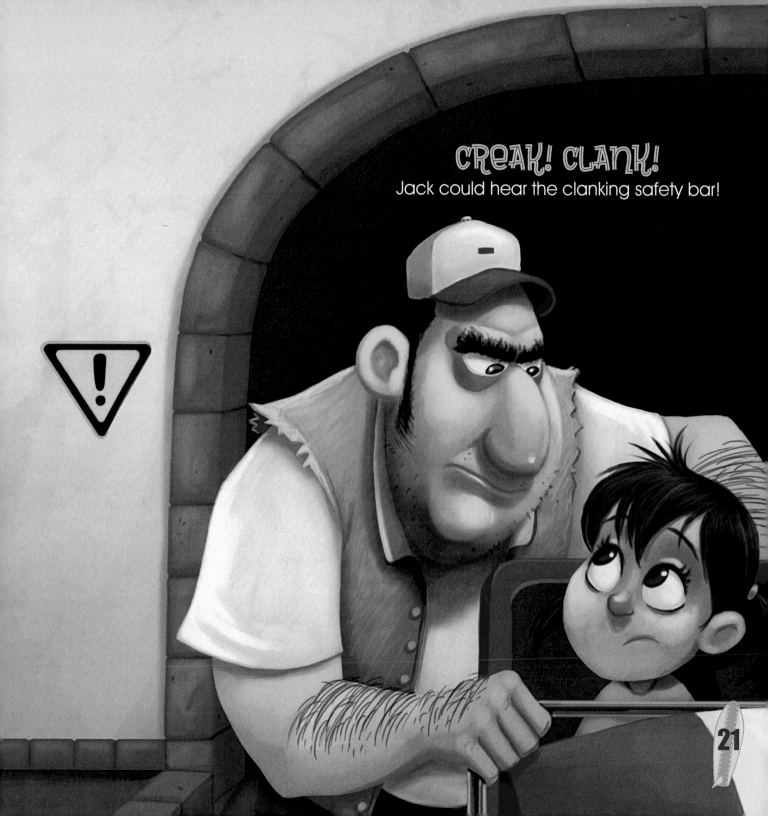

22

"Well done!" Clay beamed as he walked up to the platform and climbed into the roller coaster car.

"It's our turn?" Jack squeaked. Suddenly all the scaredies rushed back at once! As he stood on the edge of the platform, his knees were wobbly and his heart was beating extra fast.

"Step up, kid!" the ride attendant shouted.

"I-I-I can't," Jack barely whispered.

"Hey, it's OK," Clay said. "No worries. Just wait for me by the exit."

Jack nodded. But it was definitely not OK.

That night, Jack lay in bed and listened
to the wind whistle against the old beach house.
He felt so silly and scared after Big Red.

CREAK! GROAN!

"What was that?" Jack whispered. It didn't sound like wind. And those shadows on the wall looked bigger than anything in the room!

CREAK!

Jack bolted out of bed and headed for the only light that was still on.

Clay was waxing his surfboard on the back porch.

"HI, JACK!"

Jack looked down. "Hi," he mumbled. "Sorry about today. I guess the Magic Finger Countdown (MFC) doesn't work for me."

"Dude, you just have to practice! I had to do it about fifty times before I could surf." Clay looked at Jack. "Thing is...when I least expect it, I still get scared and need the MFC. Might be for killer waves. Might be for taking tests," Clay explained.

"WOW," Jack whispered. He wondered if Clay had ever been scared of the dark shadows on *his* bedroom wall.

"Look." Clay pointed to a small MFC sticker on his surfboard. "The pros put these on their boards. Because everyone needs a reminder that it's OK to feel scared."

27

"Want to try the MFC again?" Clay asked Jack the next morning. The cousins were back in line for Big Red.
"O-OK, I'll give it another try," Jack said hesitantly. He felt like his heavy backpack was on his chest "Hellooooo, heavy chest." Jack thought back to what was scary the last time.

"Hello, everyone who's staring!" Jack looked around and smiled goofily.

"Hello, grumpy-worker-guy! How do you like me now?!" Jack exclaimed.

28

"**nice.**" Clay chuckled.

Then Jack closed his fist tight and imagined all his scared feelings flowing into it.

He held it there for a minute, squeezing tighter. I've got you right where I want you, scaredies! "Captain Jack is not afraid of you!"

Jack released his fist, one finger at a time.

FIVE, FOUR, THREE, TWO...

He imagined his fears floating
away into the morning sky.

"one." Jack blew on his hand.
"Hasta la vista, scaredies!"
"Good job!" Clay said.
"Just keep doing the MFC
until it's our turn to ride."

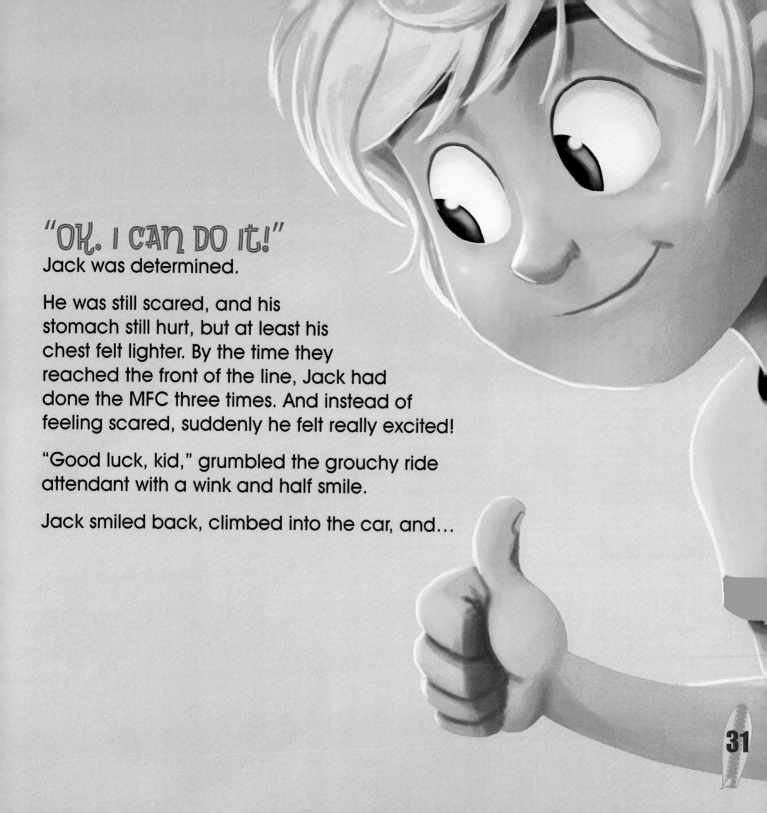

"OK. I CAN DO IT!"

Jack was determined.

He was still scared, and his stomach still hurt, but at least his chest felt lighter. By the time they reached the front of the line, Jack had done the MFC three times. And instead of feeling scared, suddenly he felt really excited!

"Good luck, kid," grumbled the grouchy ride attendant with a wink and half smile.

Jack smiled back, climbed into the car, and…

31

32

JACK RODE BIG RED!

33

"So what's next?" Jack's mom asked as she loaded his plate with his favorite homemade spaghetti and meatballs.

"What do you mean?" Jack picked up the end of a long noodle and slurped the whole thing in one, long, messy strand. His two younger cousins laughed hysterically. Jack was definitely the hero of the night.

"Well, now that you've ridden Big Red, you have to find new ways to get scared," his mom explained.

"I do?" Jack asked.

"You can't stop practicing the MFC now," Clay said. "You're totally on a roll, dude!"

Jack looked out the window toward the ocean waves and smiled mischievously.

"SURF'S UP!"

Fear and anxiety are normal and healthy emotions. They are a part of life. How we respond to that fear is what determines whether or not it will become a life-altering problem. Maybe your children struggle with the dark, noises at night, sleeping in their own beds, going to school, playing a sport, social gatherings with large crowds, spiders or snakes, fear of bodily sensations, talking in front of class, fear of rejection, fear of an angry teacher, or fear of storms/natural disasters. These are just some of the most common fears for preschool to school-age children. Be patient with children as they learn to be brave little souls. Reassure them that it is OK to feel anxious and that these feelings will pass. Help them apply Jack's story to their own lives and encourage them to practice the Magic Finger Countdown.

The Science Behind the Magic Finger Countdown

The brain's fear response center—which is partially governed by the brain's sympathetic nervous system—triggers the typical "fight or flight" response. We see this, quite literally, when children run from their beds at night. The only way to curb this stress response is to indirectly activate the brain's parasympathetic nervous system, which calls on the body to release chemicals associated with relaxation. The Magic Finger Countdown teaches the child how to do this by giving them a sense of power and control over their feelings. With repeated practice of the Magic Finger Countdown, children learn to embrace and demand more of their fears, thereby turning off the sympathetic nervous system and turning on the parasympathetic nervous system. It is, of course, science—not magic—that makes the Magic Finger Countdown work.

Tips for MFC Success:

1) **Personalize the Story**—Tailor the story and countdown to children's specific fears so they connect the technique easily to their own anxieties.

2) **Embrace & Accept It**—It is very important that they know the anxiety they feel is totally normal and that it will not hurt them. Reassure them that they are safe and that they can be totally accepting of any anxious sensation they feel. They can practice this by thinking, 'Hell-ooooo anxiety. There you are, come on in!'

3) **Release It**—As they do the Magic Finger Countdown, remind children that they are directing their fears out of their bodies, through their arm, and into their fist. When each finger extends, they are releasing fears and getting braver and stronger. It's important not to rush the Magic Finger Countdown. A slow and steady approach allows children to take control over the situation. Practice with them even when they are not anxious so they are familiar with what to do when they are anxious.

4) **Patience**—Be patient with children and practice the MFC with them until they feel comfortable doing it on their own. It may happen quickly for some and take longer for others. It is only when children have decided they've had enough of their fears, when they've crossed an imaginary line in their heads, that they'll really go for it, and the technique will work. It's up to the child—not the parent—to decide when he's ready to conquer his fears. Once they have learned to master the MFC- children will feel braver and be more willing to accept these scary sensations. They can then eventually skip step 4 of the MFC and begin practicing real acceptance. It is when children have decided they are OK with the uncomfortable feeling (accepting) and are willing to let it go, that lasting results come.

5) Demand More—If the technique does not at first seem to be working, encourage children to demand more. At the very moment when children think they can't take their fears anymore, they should stomp it out, yell it out, and get it out! Demand, in a loud voice, that the sensations do their absolute worst to scare them. This engages a stay and "fight" response rather than a quit and "flee" response. If the technique does not seem to be working on its own, encourage children to demand more. Of course, only implement the demand more technique if it is appropriate to the child's individual fear, such that there is no real danger. The more children welcome their fears and demand they do their worst, the better the result. It's counterintuitive, but it works.

6) Anger Can Be Good—Some children are at first resistant to trying the MFC. It might take an outside motivating factor, such as embarrassment when a friend learns they don't sleep in their own bed, to propel them to really work on the technique. At this point children often get angry and fed up. This anger is essential to crossing over from anger to courage. They welcome, embrace, and utilize this anger to implement the MFC.

7) Trust—Encourage children to trust their bodies and their bodies' physical reactions to fear. Learning how to be OK with the physical sensations caused by fear is a big component in retraining the brain not to recognize the fear source as something dangerous. Remind children that their bodies are able to handle these scary sensations. It is normal and OK for the sensations to continue during and after doing the MFC. Just as Clay teaches Jack in the story, the sensations will fade with practice.

8) Big Praise—Be sure to make a very impressionable big deal of your little heroes, just as Jack's mom does by making him a special meal in honor of his great achievement. Children need to know that they are courageous and strong. Let them think of themselves as brave superheroes, as this empowers them to manage their feelings on their own. You can also encourage them to feel savvy and confident by having them teach the technique to at least one younger sibling, cousin, or friend.

9) Setbacks—Expect and welcome setbacks, just as Clay tells Jack in the story. Children may be able to conquer fears one day and suddenly not be able to complete the MFC the next. These stumbles might feel scary for children, so it's important to use them as opportunities to overcome once again. They help children exercise their growing courage muscle. If framed right, setbacks can be a real confidence booster, and an essential step in mastering the Magic Finger Countdown for life.

10) Life Skill— Children can do the MFC the moment they begin to feel anxious. Some may need to complete it only a few times before doing something scary, while others may need to do the MFC before and while engaging in a scary activity. Once children have mastered the MFC, remind them that it's a tool they can access for the rest of their lives, just like the story's surf pros—who have MFC stickers on their surfboards as a reminder. They carry the MFC with them wherever they go and can use it in almost any fearful situation. Encourage them to think of it as their secret, magic tool.

BASICS OF THE MAGIC FINGER COUNTDOWN

Step One: Say "hello" to each and every one of your fears and your body's scary feelings.

Step Two: Make a fist and squeeze all of your scaredies out through your arm and into your fist.

Step Three: Squeeze your fist tight and tell your fears you have them right where you want them.

Step Four: Count down backward from five while you release one finger at a time. Blow those fears away to make sure they're gone.

Step Five: Say good-bye to your fears. Congratulate yourself on completing the technique! Trust yourself!

A NOTE FROM BARRY MCDONAGH
-best-selling author of Panic Away.

'What we resist persists'. ~Carl Jung

For the past ten years I have been helping thousands of adults end their anxiety problems with a very counter intuitive approach. This incredibly effective approach was first put forward by Dr. Viktor Frankl and later developed by Dr. Claire Weekes. In essence it teaches that when we learn to truly accept our anxiety, rather than resist it, we can heal it naturally.

I have had the great fortune of been able to share this knowledge with so many adults around the world. When I was then presented with the opportunity to co-author a children's book with Stacy Fiorile, I jumped at the chance, as I have long wanted to write something just for children.

The core technique ('Magic Finger Countdown') taught in Scaredies Away incorporates the essence of what I teach in Panic Away but in a much simpler manner for children to grasp and apply.

My hope is that any child with anxiety gets an opportunity to read this book as I think we have created something that will be of unique benefit for them.

Barry McDonagh

ABOUT THE AUTHORS

Stacy Fiorile is a Nationally Certified School Psychologist with her Masters in Counseling and Continued Advanced Graduate Study. Stacy is a graduate from Montclair State University and Georgian Court University. She has studied anxiety and panic in depth on both a personal and professional level for the past fourteen years. She is committed to improving the lives of children in the area of good mental health through her writing and work as a School Psychologist.

Barry McDonagh is a graduate in Arts with a Diploma in Psychology. He is the creator of the well known and very successful program Panic Away. The program has been purchased by more than 70,000 people worldwide and has been featured on TV and radio across America. In addition, Barry has an online audience of more than 200,000 people with whom he communicates regularly through his monthly newsletters.

To view endorsements and testimonials for the panic away program and for more on Barry's latest work go to www.panicaway.com

For more on Stacy and her work to date, visit www.panicaway.com/kids

Don't forget!
Get your free bonus audio for
this book by visiting
www.panicaway.com/kids
Enter the code: AMZ19

What people are saying about Scaredies Away:

essential for kids everywhere!

"Perfect book for helping your child get to sleep on those certain nights when there seems to be shadows everywhere!" –**Donal Scannell**

Perfect for Parents and Kids

"I liked the simple way of explaining the method. I will suggest it to parents of small kids. Would love to have this when I was a kid!!!!!!" –**Kilo Marsellos**

"This illustrated kids' book will help young ones handle their panic. The simple steps for identifying, acknowledging and releasing fear offer a useful method for helping younger children move past panic into a place of confidence…high-quality, vibrant illustrations provide an appealing mix of wide-eyed energy and bobble-headed attitude…colorful cartoon characters in a tidy five-step program for anxious pre-adolescents… anxiety can be transformed into a sense of personal power. " -**Kirkus Review**

A Must Read!

"I would recommend this book for every family with children! Believe me parents you can learn something as well as you teach your child you have added a new tool to your emotional tool box! as a Personal Life coach I will use and share it daily!" -**Peg Beaton**

"I bought this book for my son to help with some of his anxiety issues and i read it myself and found it to help with my anxiety also, very pleased with this purchase." –**Sara Corey**

Awesome! Highly Recommended

"I purchased this book because genetically, for centuries, my biological family has dealt with severe anxiety. I wanted this DNA issue to be understood and handled properly. For myself, my children and my grandchildren I knew there just had to be a solution! This book teaches us all, no matter the age, how to easily handle those scardy feelings we have without allowing them to control our lives and stop us from living our lives to the fullest! I give this wonderful book 5 stars! A+! Very entertaining, well written, educational and enlightening! It has now become my 4 year old Grandsons favorite book! He used to be so scared of the dark and to sleep in his own room, but now he takes the book to bed with him to remind himself that he is in control over those old scary feelings. Now he is happy and feels like a super hero! Excellent indeed!" –**Michelle Anne Cox-Iomas-Review Maven**

Great Book

"An excellent tool for children which explains how to deal with anxieties. Easy to understand and apply the concepts to any situation." -**Mscheel**

"Beautifully illustrated Scaredies Away! is an important book dealing with childhood anxiety….I was fascinated with the simplicity of the presentation and it's easy to comprehend techniques… This will serve as a reference or a guide for me …. Scaredies Away! is a must have book in our book shelves. " -**A Timeline of Destiny blog review**

PARENT EDUCATOR SAYS THUMBS UP
For This Book On Anxiety In Children

"Children get scared. And if their fears are not coped with in childhood, they follow them into adulthood and affect relationships, professionally and personally. I have worked with Barry's Panic Away program for some years and recommended it to individuals who needed additional assistance. I am grateful for this additional tool to have to share with global families on dealing with panic, fear and anxiety." **-Judy Helm Wright, author and parent educator**

EVERY CHILD SHOULD READ THIS BOOK
"My nine year old grandson was born worried! He always seems to have some happening or other in his life - a thunderstorm, school, etc., - that spoils his enjoyment of the day. We read this book together and he loved it, told his mum and younger sister how to do the magic finger count. They read the book the next night and both used the count to keep their scaredies away. I don't know yet if it will keep working and help him get control of his worries, but at least it is a start ,and I think he loved the idea that other kids have the same problem .Thank you so much for writing and publishing this book." **–Linet M. King**

"SCAREDIES AWAY" IS HELPING MY GRANDSON
 "I bought this book because I felt it would give my grandson tools to use to overcome some personal fears he has. Yesterday he read the book to me. He enjoyed it and afterward he tried out the finger count down technique. When his Dad came to pick him up my grandson showed him what he had learned to do if he was feeling afraid. But the best part of all of this time he and I had together, was that, before his Dad came to get him, we talked about some fears that he had because the book showed him that everyone has fears about something. I shared how I felt when I was a child and had to deal with the same things that make him afraid now. He had a time of feeling bad about being afraid, but the book was what helped him to realize that it was a normal feeling that everyone feels at one time or another. When we were done sharing, he was feeling happy and like he knew he had a tool to help him conquer his fears! **-Modell**

"Awesome book really helpful teaching tool! Parents around the world should get a copy of it the science behind it is great!" **-Zack**

WORTH THE PRICE
"I wish I would have had this as a child and learned the finger countdown. Didn't have my 1st full on panic attack until 19yo, but always had anxiety as a child. I think if a parent would have done this with me and worked on it until I had it down, It may have curtailed my current anxiety disorder. So worth the price for your children......way cheaper than counseling! (Good for adults too)."
–Amy Slate

"When I read it to my son he connected with the characters almost immediately. The book was very engaging in that my son counted along with the boys to rid them of their "scaredies". He was worried that the kids at school wouldn't recognize him with his new haircut. So on our way to school he counted and poof, there was that smile."

WISH I HAD THIS WHEN I WAS A CHILD

My friend said when reading it to her son, he was very engaged and listened intently. What a fantastic tool to help children in today's fast paced environment. Anything that can help children cope with anxiety and engage them definitely get my thumbs up!
-Miss Megan J. Phillips

"The back of the book has very helpful tips and insights for parents to better understand anxiety which I think is awesome. I really, we really liked this book and I would recommend it to any parent who is looking for a way to help their child cope with worry and anxiety."
-makemommygosomethingsomething blog review

GOOD BOOK

I can't wait to have my granddaughter read the book. I hope she can use the technique to help her when she worries. I have used it a couple times myself. –Jane Brehe

"We have read Scaredies Away as a bedtime story several times and my son, who is usually happy to let his sister do the bedtime story choosing, has requested it many more times."- Bury Family Life
- The Family magazine for Bury, Lancashire UK

KIDS LOVE IT

I gave my purchases to my siblings who told me their kids love the story and the MFC is wonderful experience the kids enjoy. –Jin Tee Png

"If only my parents had known what to do about my fears back then, I wouldn't have suffered for over 40 years. Scaredies Away! is a great place for parents to start. And kids will love the characters, colors and art. I loved that the older, popular boy said he had been scared too-letting the child know he is not alone." -Polly Meyers Co-Founder "Break Free From Anxiety"

My grandchildren loved the book ...gave them a special way to deal with fear. Adults can use the same techniques to overcome moments of anxiety or the fear of fear. -Fran

BRILLIANT FOR CHILDREN

I have given this book a five star rating because anxiety in children especially in Christchurch after the earthquakes is very high and I think this book would be exactly what they need. –Sandra Pilet

My granddaughter has not read this yet because I purchased it as a gift for this coming Christmas. But I have read it and think the technique make is very easy to follow and will help my granddaughter when she gets scared at night. I would highly recommend this book for children. -Ann

MY MFC GOAL SHEET

1. _____

2. _____

3. _____

4. _____

5. _____

6. _____

7. _____

8. _____

9. _____

10. _____

Made in the USA
San Bernardino, CA
03 July 2018